T0065966

TO MAKE IT RIGHT

TO MAKE IT RIGHT

Poems by

Corrinne Clegg Hales

Autumn House Press

Pittsburgh

Autumn House Press Staff
Editor-in-Chief and Founder: Michael Simms
Executive Director: Richard St. John
Co-Founder: Eva-Maria Simms
Community Outreach Director: Michael Wurster
Fiction Editors: Sharon Dilworth, John Fried
Associate Editors: Ziggy Edwards, Erik Rosen, Rebecca King
Assistant Editor: Adrienne Block
Media Consultant: Jan Beatty
Publishing Consultant: Peter Oresick
Editorial Consultant: Thom Ward
Technology Consultant: Evan Oare
Tech Crew Chief: Michael Milberger
Intern: D. Gilson

ISBN: 978-1-932870-47-3
Library of Congress Control Number: 2010918172

Autumn House Press receives state arts funding support through a grant from the Pennsylvania Council on the Arts, a state agency funded by the Commonwealth of Pennsylvania and the National Endowment for the Arts, a federal agency.

for John,
and in memory of Blanche Cox Clegg

Acknowledgements

I'm very grateful to the following journals for first publishing these poems (sometimes in slightly different versions or with different titles):

Arts & Letters: "'Young Nubian Woman'"
Blackbird: "Disappeared: From a Photograph by Gustave
                         LeGray"
                         "Critical Care"
                         "Firewood"
BorderSenses: "Flight"
Cortland Review: "To Make it Right"
Hudson Review: "Medea"
In the Grove: "The Glassblower's Breath"
The Ledge: "American Art"
                         "Clarity: Because I'm Not There"
Mississippi Review: "Trajectory"
Nimrod: "Dead Finch in the Parsley"
                         "Hectograph: Words Rising"
                         "Late Summer Moratorium"
Northwest Review: "Forgiven"
                         "City Cemetery Love Poem:1975"
                         "Failed Blessing"
Notre Dame Review: "Remission of Sin"
Packinghouse Review :"Accidental Revelation: August 1999"
                         "Forensics"
                         "Unburied"
                         "Clothesline Shopper"
Ploughshares: "School Lunch Work Program"
Poetry East: "Unsolved"
Quarterly West: "What Actually Happens"
Southern Review: "Sunday Morning"

Several poems also appeared in *Out of This Place*, a chapbook published by March Street Press

All picnics are eaten on the grave.

—Adrienne Rich

Contents

IV. Trajectory

I. What Actually Happens

Hectograph: Words Rising

My mother struggles for a word
she's known all her life, and her fingers
move to her mouth as if to pull
the word from her body
like a thorn, but she waits—
just as she used to wait
for the words to appear in her
homemade copy machine.
She'd boil sugar and gelatin in water, add
glycerin, stirring down the foam
in wide circles, and finally pour
the syrupy concoction
into a flat roasting pan to cool. She'd type
a page full of purple words
and place the carbon face down
onto the transparent surface of gelatin.
When the words had sunk in
deep enough, she'd spread a white sheet
of paper on top, smooth it
with the back of a serving spoon,
and we'd all wait for her words
to swim back up through the wobbly medium
onto the page—which she'd hold up
for our amazement, printed as clear and bold
as anything—and soon the tables and chairs,
even the floor, would be covered
with pages drying, words hung
everywhere, cooked up like supper
from her hand to our mouths.

The Rich

When she finally got him to agree,
my brother brought the chosen pigeon
to my mother headless, dripping
all over the floor, and dropped it
in the sink. He was twelve,
and didn't want tenderness
messing up his life. His pigeons
nested in the shed out back
above the empty rabbit hutches,
and hadn't been contributing
their fair share. Animals,
my father insisted, are for food
or work or sale. No pets. No feeding
animal mouths before our own.
So our mother kept telling us
how the rich eat squab—how
squab is a delicacy—*squab under glass*—
she'd say, making an elaborate dome shape
with her hands in the air. *And squab is—*
believe it or not—just another word
for pigeon. She'd click her tongue
and shrug whenever she said this
as if the foolish rich had fallen
for some easy-to-see-through scam.
She plucked and gutted and washed
and stuffed, and when she called us
to the table it was sitting there hot
and brown, no bigger than a sparrow,
smack in the middle
of a sea-green Melmac plate,

under a clear glass mixing bowl,
a ragged sprig of spearmint
plopped flat on its breast
and bread crumbs tumbling out
from between its tiny crossed legs.
She was smiling. *The rich*, she said,
pay big bucks for a meal
like this, and when she lifted the glass,
all seven of us gathered around,
imagining we were them—breathing
the abundant odor of onion
and pulling slivers of meat
from the carcass with our fingers.

Sunday Morning

Crowded around the glowing open mouth
of the electric oven, the children
pull on clothes and eat brown-sugared oatmeal.

The broiler strains, buzzing to keep up
500 degrees, and the mother
is already scrubbing at a dark streak

on the kitchen wall. Last night she'd been
ironing shirts and trying her best to explain
something important to the children

when the old mother cat's surviving
two kittens' insistent squealing and scrambling
out of their cardboard box began

to get to her. The baby screamed every time
the oldest girl set him on the cold floor
while she carried a kitten back to its place

near the stove, and the mother cat kept reaching
for the butter dish on the table. Twice, the woman
stopped talking and set her iron down to swat

a quick kitten away from the dangling cord,
and she saw that one of the boys had begun to feed
margarine to his favorite by the fingerful.

When it finally jumped from his lap and squatted
to piss on a long-sleeved shirt dropped below

her ironing board, the woman calmly stopped, unplugged

her iron, picked up the gray kitten with one hand
and threw it, as if it were a housefly, hard
and straight at the yellow flowered wall

across the room. It hit, cracked, and seemed to slide
into a heap on the floor, leaving an odd silence
in the house. They all stood still

staring at the thing, until one child,
the middle boy, walked slowly out of the room
and down the hall without looking

at his mother or what she'd done. The others followed
and by morning everything was back to normal
except for the mother, standing there scrubbing.

What Actually Happens

Her seven kids are locked outside again. When Carla cleans
her house, she needs to be alone. These frenzies seem to hit her

without warning—whirlwind of ammonia, Clorox, rag, broom,
brush. We can almost hear her scrubbing through the walls. The oldest

daughter will be pregnant soon—at fourteen she'll have to choose
whether to run off with a grim-faced boy who pumps gas weekends

and drives a pickup truck, or to add another open mouth
to her mother's increasing madness. Carla loves her children

fiercely—she gives them dish detergent bubble baths and sings to them
at night. She sings Patsy Cline and the Everly Brothers, and the children

sing along. She promises them everything—they dream of bicycles,
t-bone steak and faraway places they'll never see, and she forgives them

all their sins. But there's never enough food or room
in the house, and none of the men ever stay long enough

to make any difference at all. The last man
seemed likely, but objected when the kids came shuffling

into bed in the middle of every night, snuggling up against
Carla's warm back or his own, throwing their small, damp arms or legs

over his belly as casually as if he were a puppy
or a lover. And he objected in the first place to the way she'd let them fall

asleep anywhere in the house, dropping like rain-wasted blossoms
onto sticky linoleum floors. More than once he'd tripped,

on his way to an early morning piss, over a small child's body, curled
like an animal on the cool bathroom floor.

Carla's caseworker tells her not to sleep with men
for money, so she asks them to bring pizza, or take-out chicken

or hamburgers for the kids. And the caseworker wants to see
clean floors and faces—no piles of laundry or buckets of rotting diapers

or bowls of half-eaten macaroni around the house. It gets to be
overwhelming. My sister and I have seen her toss

all the dirty clothes into grocery bags and burn them, starting over
with one new outfit for each child when the welfare check

came in. It was the boldest thing we could imagine—burning
all your clothes—and on the hottest day last summer, in the last week

of July when no one's mother had any money left, Carla put on
her enormous flowered housecoat, piled

ten or twelve stray kids into her old green Ford, and drove straight
to the Safeway store where she told us to wait in the car in the heat.

When she emerged empty-handed, we wailed as if we were dying.
Carla just smiled and started the car. After the second stoplight,

she shifted into third and began pulling bright popsicles from her dress
and tossing them crazily, two and three at a time

over her shoulder, over the back seat, into our sweaty, happy hands.
I know this morning's cleaning frenzy won't change the future,

and neither will the sweetness of the stolen popsicles,
but these things are at least as true

as what actually happens. Next winter the newest baby—
the one born on Carla's kitchen table with only my mother

and another neighbor woman to help clean up—will slip underneath
the soapy tub-water one afternoon, after all her brothers

have jumped out, forgetting their sister in their rush, and Carla
will be sipping her black coffee slowly at the bare kitchen window,

eyes closed, savoring such unusual silence, when
she finally thinks to check. I remember her shrieking,

running out into the cold gravel street barely hanging on
to the fat baby's body, soap suds still sliding off her skin.

School Lunch Work Program

As soon as she cleans her tray, she stops
by the office, picks up a grocery bag
marked with her name in red crayon

and spends the rest of her lunch cleaning
paper scraps, twigs, leaves, and other trash
from the school's scrubby patch

of front lawn. She does this diligently,
no complaints, as if it were class work,
finishing before the bell, missing

nothing. After a couple of weeks,
when the lawn is free
of every scrap, the girl is reduced to

walking back and forth, eyes
on the ground, waiting
for something to fall or blow in

off the street. Noontime traffic passes by,
muffled playground shouts
and giggles dissolve like a foreign language

at her feet. Finally a man in a pickup truck
brakes for a red light and tosses
a crumpled cigarette pack out

his open window onto the sidewalk
where the girl stands holding

her paper bag. I think it was

a Camels pack--white, brown, foil-lined—
and the grim child reaching down, grabbing
at other people's garbage, might have been me.

Thirty years have torn the building
down, transformed that school yard nicely
into a brightly lit McDonald's

hamburger stand, and has molded me
into a respectable citizen
alive and well in another state,

but time and distance have done nothing
with the lump of cold shame that rides
chronically under my belt, always threatening

to turn suddenly malignant.
A high-heeled teacher passes by smiling
and a classmate jumps

out of his mother's shiny car, spitting
a bright pink wad of bubble gum onto the lawn
as he runs for his place

on the playground. Straightening up,
the girl suddenly knows for sure
she will never eat lunch

at school again. From now on she will say
she isn't hungry, that she ate
breakfast at home, and she'll go directly

from class to playground—the school's hot lunch
wasn't so great anyway. I'm trying
to be accurate about this. Maybe it wasn't me

at all—maybe I am the boy who spit
a nickel's worth of bubble gum onto the grass. I paid
for my lunches a week in advance, and today

my mother took me for ice cream because
I did well on a test and I deserved
a special treat. Maybe at ten years old

I already know the value
of a dollar, and if other kids can't pay
their own way, they ought to earn the price

of lunch by working it off. Maybe my father
gives me a hefty allowance every Saturday
and a dollar for every respectable mark

on my report card. Maybe I have a warm
winter coat and I could choose
to bring ham sandwiches to school

if I wanted to. But one of us is picking up
that sloppy wad of gum, and it feels

«13»

warm, sticky, full of germs—there is no way

to get it off your hands. You wipe it onto the inside
of the paper bag, rub your fingers on your clothes,
finally put them one at a time into your mouth,

lick the slimy sweetness off your skin
and swallow. Something has started to grow
inside this girl's belly. She walks to the street, sits

carefully on the cold cement curb, begins
tearing the paper trash bag methodically into useless
pieces. She saves the part with her red name

until last, ripping each letter separately
into waxy shreds, filling the gutter
with a fluffy paper pile. Just as the bell rings

giving her permission to re-enter
the building, she pulls a kitchen match
from her jacket pocket, strikes it

on the curb and lights a small, fast fire
that burns hot and feels good.
Cars honk and a few drivers shout,

but she continues to sit perfectly
still, watching her own fire,
and by the time the principal rushes

out, ashes are already blowing
into the street, leaving the darkened gutter
empty and astonishingly clean.

To Make it Right

Crouched low in my dank pool
of rage, I waited behind
the wooden fence until she walked
through the gate. She was
bigger than me, but slower,
and I sprang up, slamming
deep into her belly with both fists,
over and over with more force
than I believed my body
could produce. She collapsed, hard
and heavy as a wet pair of jeans
might drop from a clothesline, but she didn't
look angry or afraid. She stared at me
with what seemed like awe
before she stopped falling and began
to cry—not loudly, as I expected—
but softly, almost weeping, sitting there
in a pale clump of her mother's
spent daffodils, arms wrapped
around her knees. I could hear
a dog barking in the yard
next door, and someone's car
starting, as if nothing had happened,
and I just stood there, hands hanging
stupidly above her, trembling
with what should have been
shame, wanting her to stand,
to strike back, to make it right.

Remission of Sin

Barely out of high school and given the power
to deliver new life, he stands in loose
white clothing, waist high
in consecrated water, accepting
each child into his hands. Nine children
lined up this morning, all dressed in white—

or nearly white—pajamas, pushed
by devoted mothers toward the pool.
The boy tries to stay focused
on the work, head bowed, left hand low
on the child's back, right holding both her hands
in front of her chest, the memorized prayer,

then the gentle pressure
until she is swept off her feet
and he pushes her head under
absolving all previous sins. Last night,
on the wide bench seat of his Ford pickup truck,
right arm around the shoulders of the girl

he'd taken to the movies, his left hand began
sliding under her skirt, moving slowly
to the inside of her thigh. This time
she hadn't stopped him, and they tended
to each other's skin as if touch
were salvation. Immersion

must be absolute, so he looks closely
along the submerged child's body

for strands of floating hair, a knee popping up—
a single toe surfacing invalidates the act.
He wonders if he has made his own body
too unclean be an agent of God,

worries that he might be
transmitting sin like disease
every time he raises a child, sputtering
and slipping, from the water into the air,
but he goes on saying the words,
breathing them out over each small, shivering body,

looking into their shut-eyed faces
through holy water, seeing how they trust
his strong basketball-playing hands
to place them in danger and bring them back again,
and he thinks of his father tossing him
into the dark middle of an irrigation pond

when he was seven, telling him
he'd better learn to save himself, telling him
no one else would do it for him. He remembers
how he struggled, swallowing
what seemed like gallons of slimy pond water
before he finally thrashed his way

to the side and crawled up through the mud
into his father's solitary approval.
Tonight, after dark, he and the girl will talk
as they touch, and they will take each other

to all the damp, private places
of their bodies, and back again, trusting

in each other's hands, each other's mouths,
each other's breath. This last child is nervous,
one hand pinching her nose, the other
clinging white to his wrist. The boy can feel
the strings of her muscles begin to pull
into panic at the small of her back.

As he pushes her under, her eyes blink open,
her dark hair flowers around her head.

Clothesline Shopper

Have you ever stolen anything? If so, why?
—question on a mental health evaluation

It wasn't on a dare, or some type of gang
initiation, or even a cry
for parental attention—and it certainly wasn't

for the thrill—as with Winona Ryder,
or the affluent but unnamed
girl in the Oates short story. It wasn't even need,

really. We had clothes. The ladies from church
brought us a grocery bag of used skirts and blouses
and socks they collected every fall

when school was about to start,
and we'd watch our mother say thank you,
thank you at the door. So each time

my sister and I rode our dilapidated bicycle
across town, me pedaling, her straddling
the back fender, bare feet sticking out

in both directions; each time we slipped into the clean
swept streets of the suburbs, a pillowcase flying
from a knot on the handle bars; each time we hovered, invisible

as dust, between straight brick houses, scanning
green backyards for the right laundry hung out
to dry; each time we finally dropped the bike

to the curb under an elm tree or an oak, jumped
a tall, squared-off hedge and fell into
the backyard of another world—we didn't think

about why. We'd simply start pulling
blue jeans from the line, sending sprung halves
of clothespins flying up like fat moths, every which way,

stuffing bright shirts and soft underwear
into our bag, until we couldn't stop laughing
and one of us would hoist the plump pillowcase

over a shoulder, and we'd scramble
back into the street. We weren't angry
at the girls who lived in those houses—we admired

the way they called out to each other
as they walked down the halls
at school, the way their bracelets jingled

when they raised their hands in class, the way
their ponytails bounced back and forth—
and how the teachers seemed to love them, giving

them hall passes with a smile and nodding
approval when they spoke. And we especially loved
the sweet smell rising in the stairwell

as they passed by.

Janitor

I believe now that we were sent there
so our grandfather wouldn't be alone all night
cleaning the enormous movie theater,

so he wouldn't be alone two-thirds of the way
up an aluminum extension ladder
the next time his heart closed up

and knocked him to the floor,
so there would be someone—even a child—
to call home or an ambulance, to unbutton

the top button of his gray work shirt,
so he wouldn't have to lie
gasping for hours in the greasy heaps

of popcorn he'd just swept
from between the rows, breathing
oily residue and syrup spills

and movie-goer squalor. He'd been rescued
the last time by the nineteen-year-old
projectionist coming in before noon

to splice a broken film just in time
for the midday matinee, and because
there was no other choice, he was back

at work in two weeks. I was eight
and happy to be hired to crawl
with my sister up and down

each row of seats, picking through trash
for coins and combs, and anything heavy
or valuable or stuck to the floor. He'd follow,

dragging the heavy electric blower, yelling at us
to go faster, creating little whirlwinds
of paper cups and popcorn that worked their way

down the raked floor toward the screen
where he could scoop it all into trash bins
and haul it out the door. He'd let us keep

any money we found and half-eaten boxes
of candy if it looked reasonably clean,
but the rest of our treasures had to wait

weeks before he'd finally be allowed
to bring home the bin of combs and barrettes
and rings—sometimes even a sweater

or a scarf, or a handkerchief embroidered
with a girl's initials. The old man hardly spoke
those nights—we'd work in silence—

my sister and I thinking about tomorrow
when we'd get into the movie for free,
sit in the dark in these same seats, watching

and listening for what was already falling,
waiting for us on the concrete floor.

Forgiven

—for the boy who asked me to pray with him after sex

I knew what we were going to do
when you down-shifted and turned
onto Millcreek Canyon Road, when you

parked at a gravel turnout overlooking
the hazy sparkle of city lights, when you unrolled
all the windows so we could see

Jupiter and the swollen moon and breathe in
the dampness of dogwood blossoms, when
you cranked the old Rambler's seats back

as far as they would go, when we fell together
into the soft blanket, sighing and humming,
when we let our tongues move into each other's

mouths and ears, when we let our hands slide
under cotton, onto skin. I knew what we were
going to do when you pulled your shirt

off over your head, when I
unbuttoned mine. So, afterward,
when you began to cry

so unexpectedly, covering your face
with your crumpled shirt, asking me why
I let you do it, when you

got down on your knees right there
on the side of the road and asked god
to forgive us for the amazing thing

we'd just done, I pulled my clothes together
and started walking, descending the dark miles
with blouse still flapping open, past other

parked cars and the sweet sounds
of the unrepentant lovers inside them, and past
the coldness of the creek and the shadowy

aspens, and I kept moving downward
toward the well-lighted city, where I'd hitch a ride
at the highway, and the goodhearted driver

would take one look as I climbed in—
tucking and buttoning, and smoothing
my hair—and ask what happened, assuming

I'd been, at the very least, roughed up
by my date. I do hope you felt forgiven
that night, but I want you to know now

that it's taken all these years
for me to recall the astonishing heat
of your hands on my face and the way

our breathing became a song, how we

could feel our bones pressing right through
our skin, and how we seemed to be

floating, rising, transparent as smoke
for those few fragrant moments
before your prayer.

II. Some Place to Go

Medea

—after a sketch by Peter Paul Rubens

After all the silent waiting, she streaks by
so fast that her body makes a crescent, head
thrown back, hair flying, clothes trailing, mouth
warped into a long howl, a child's
limp body tucked under her arm
like a package. She strides across the world
until she becomes nothing
but a single bare arm, muscular
and resolute as the irresistible arm of god, pulling
the older boy along by his wrist
as any mother might
drag a resistant child from the playground
at dinner time. Finally, near the edge,
she looks at us, exhausted
but not slowing, both spent children
now firmly in her grip, the smallest
a loose bundle of rags
held close to her waist,
the other dangling heavily
from her hand
on the other side. She will never
let them go. How does hopelessness
gather such force? If you didn't know
the story, you might think this is hope—
that she is rescuing these children
from disaster—escaping
a burning house or an earthquake,

a bad husband or a war. You might believe
help is on the way, you might imagine
she has some place to go.

Hunger

That fall, when her husband kills the deer and her marriage
　is coming apart for good, she decides to butcher it
by herself on a board on the kitchen floor.

One quarter at a time, she hauls the carcass in
　from where it has been hanging in the garage, scrapes it
and saws and cuts according to a diagram

in the book propped open in front of her: rump roast, rib roast,
　chuck, sirloin, brisket, shanks, ribs. The deer is as big as she is,
and at first it seems strange to be working with a knife inside

a hollowed-out body like this, but she gets used to the sharp,
　metallic smell, and the cool feel of the flesh and even the sound
of the bones cracking when, after sawing halfway through,

she has to break them apart with her hands.
　The first thing she'd seen, when her husband burst through
the back door, was the blood-soaked belly-pouch

of his sweatshirt. For a split second, she thought
　he might have been shot in the stomach
himself, but he pulled out a dark deer liver and heart

slapped them on the table and smiled. Outside, the body
　of a beautiful four-point buck was stretched along the bed
of his pickup truck, its head dangling oddly over

the open tailgate's edge. Now her two small children
　crouch in the doorway watching while she pushes and pulls

her hacksaw through shiny tendons and into bone

dislocating shoulders and hips; they watch her slide knife-edge
   along steel to sharpen it, and they see their mother
making the meat into smaller, more manageable pieces.

She works hard, wiping her bloody hands on her shirt
   and paying no attention to the mess she's made. At the end,
she clamps the heavy food grinder onto the counter's edge

and, piece by piece, mixing in slick handfuls
   of beef suet as she goes, she feeds every last scrap of flesh
through the blades, making perfect pound-sized swirls

for the children to break apart
   and flatten into fat round patties she will fry
with peppers and sweet onions for their supper.

She weighs and wraps each piece carefully in white
   butcher paper, tapes it, labels it and tucks it
neatly into the freezer against the future

she knows none of them will have.

The Glassblower's Breath

I can almost see his breath
    through the blurred green glass
of this antique float, all that's left
    of one person a century
after death. I wonder
    if he thought of his work
as art--if he sighed as he set
    each globe to cool, pleased to have made
a beautiful thing—or if it was
    simply more work,
like stacking crates or sweeping
    floors. Strung together, the floats
must have looked like clusters
    of fish eggs, riding on the sea, holding
their heavy nets up and open wide,
    biding their time. Here, in my backyard
pond, a single green globe
    carries the blower's ancient breath
in slow circles, a fragile
    casket, on fire in the morning sun.
The big fish nose around, pushing,
    shoving, nibbling, and the dark fry
dart into the dense roots
    of a water hyacinth or the tangle
of parrot feather sprouting
    on the surface, hiding from their own
parents' appetites. Each spring, I watch
    new fish hatch in a shallow dish
of pond water under a microscope
    in my kitchen. The eggs are clear

amber orbs at first, then two huge eyes
        like dark yolks appear, then a thin line
that will become vein and spine
        and motion. The creature
defines itself as you watch: a tail
        materializes, twitches, begins to push
at the confines of the egg. Curled
        tight, it seems all eyes and tail,
then suddenly you are aware
        of a pulse, a pink smear
of a heart, telegraphing
        its urgent message of platelets
along the vein, and the thing flips,
        thrashes until it bursts the skin of the egg
and wriggles out, transparent
        as glass, not a fish yet—but something
hungry and alive. The glassblower
        had to know just how much molten glass
to scoop onto the pipe's end, just how hard
        to blow. His breath would push
the hot, glowing blob out into its thinning
        roundness, make a soft whooshing
or humming inside the long pipe, and when
        he sealed off the end, his breath
would be caught, sound and all, in this
        new translucent body. If it breaks,
I'm afraid he will disappear, die again,
        or maybe he will be reborn, halfway
around the world from where
        he started, sucking in air,

defining the full shape of his lungs, his heart,
      his flesh, and blowing it all back
one long breath at a time.

Critical Care

She could be a puppet, blue strings trailing
from the backs of her hands, her index finger,
her nose, her mouth, even her crotch,

but her wrists are strapped to the metal
bed rails, also her ankles, and white tape
covers her mouth like a burglar's gag

keeping the respirator tube in place.
If she could see herself like this, splayed out
under a thin sheet surrounded

by shower curtains and stainless steel
and everything on wheels, she might laugh.
But she is thinking now of learning to swim

in a slow, dirty river, remembering
how her brother dared her to dive
between his legs, and when she did,

how he clenched her head with his knees
and held her there thrashing,
hitting at him through the water

until there were knives in her lungs.
It's cold here. She can't speak
or feel or move a finger.

She can't even open her eyes. A voice
tells her *morphine*, a voice says *curare*,

it says *don't worry. It will wear off soon.*

This is all so normal for them—
they strap people down and knock people out
and string people up like this

every day. They do it to save them.
The woman waits. She thinks
she has forgotten how to breathe. She hears

someone gasping from a bed
behind the curtain—loud, clumsy breaths
far apart, the strange deep brand of breathing

that the dying do—as if to prove
they can still do it, as if the air itself
might grab them by the shoulders

and shake them back to life.

"Young Nubian Woman"

It is a matter of persuading them to pose,
which they fear doing . . . .
 —Pierre Trémaux, 1850s

Her bare feet flat
on stone pavement, she faces
the camera almost naked.
She must be very young,
no hips, no waist, breasts
barely budding on her chest.
This is probably Egypt,
the exhibit note says, and the girl
was brought here as a slave
from central Africa.
She is caught again
at this moment on salted paper
which will give her eternal life
in European galleries
and art books, and keep her
at this age—safe as she will ever be.
It's a kind of seduction, really,
convincing the girl that she won't be
hurt, that she might even like it,
and placing her body just how
he wants it, gently, even tenderly,
and then asking her to be
completely still. Don't move.
This is how I want you

to stay forever. Please
don't move a hair. I wonder
why she complies, what she's
thinking, and I wonder what
the photographer wants me
to see in this girl. I think
of that other photo, a hundred years
later, of a girl about this age
running, screaming, her body
on fire, down a war-pitted road
halfway around the world,
and the four seconds of film
from another war, taken
of a young mother on Saipan
who looked at a camera mounted
on a rifle stock and believed
the photographer aimed to kill her,
or worse, and in fact, he catches her
running toward the cliff
and keeps filming as she throws
her two babies and then
her own panic-driven body
into the sea, and the camera
pans down to the corpse
of a child being battered
in the water and rocks
like dirty laundry. And my own
daughter's slim body at eleven
or twelve, how we wanted
to believe her life

was on the verge of becoming
her own—but I'm looking now
at this African girl, dark hair
chopped into straight lines
framing her face. She stares
into the future, one hand splayed
against the ancient rock wall
behind her. She stiffens,
bracing herself for the long
exposure, and her shadow,
that deformed echo,
slides down the wall.

Disappeared: from a Photograph by Gustave LeGray

*. . . a woman moved during the exposure, resulting
in a blur at the center of the photograph.*
—exhibit note, Getty Museum

Because she disobeyed,
she's disappeared, leaving only this ghost
beside her husband, who hasn't noticed yet,
he is so intent on his own lasting image.
A rifle slung over one shoulder, he seems to be
smoking a pipe, but it's hard to be certain
of anything in this small print of travelers
on a French river bank. Everyone
holds still but her. Maybe she turned
to look back, like Lot's wife,
at where she had come from, maybe
she simply heard a sound: a dog barking
or a pheasant scared up from the grass, and for that
transgression, she dissolves into her private
future, while the others stay behind, stopped
in this static eternity, like the patient
out cold on an operating table, perfectly clear
in another photo, a team of surgeons
hovering over him as indistinct
as angels, faceless, refusing to be saved
by stillness themselves, but understanding
that if you want to be saved,
you have to die in some way first,
as in the ironic pact with god that has us
agreeing to death as prerequisite

for eternal life. Maybe ghosts are nothing
but resistance, and this disappearing
woman's body has become a ghost
because it could not stop—
even for the shutter's few seconds—
responding to the call of this world.

Flight

On the sloped eaves of the adjoining roof outside
      this third floor office window, a pair of fat pigeons
have nested on top of the decomposing
      corpse of another pigeon. Its bony head protrudes
from beneath the haphazard pile of twigs
      and leaves that don't quite bury it, and the whole mess
seems about to slide right off the roof, a small,
      strange storm, onto the busy heads of students
walking below. One pigeon, the gray-violet color
      of a bruise, sits with two scraggly hatchlings waiting
for her mate to bring food and relieve her watch—
      and you watch that happen, the clumsy
hopping out and in, the flap of one taking
      the other's place, and you wonder
who the dead bird is to them, a first partner?
      a parent? a simple opportunity? Do they even know it
from the scant materials they've brought here
      in their own mouths? They feed their squawking
young in turns, perched awkwardly on a ridge
      of sheet metal, or the thin windowsill meant
only for trim. There's no way to reach them, the thick
      office window doesn't open, so you see this scene
four feet away, every morning, become
      intimate, and strangely accustomed to the decay
and the regurgitative feeding, and the swelling bodies
      of the young. You watch them nudge
and shift, and settle into the sinking pile of feathers
      and once in awhile, what's left of a wing
lifts a little, its efficient form still responding,
      without direction or purpose,
to the slightest turn of air.

American Art

Someone has painted a human figure
on the decomposing underbelly

of an ancient car wreck. I think it's a Hudson,
built before I was born, abandoned

decades ago in this ravine where it landed
on one crushed side after its driver

swerved to avoid a deer, or a ghost,
and careened over the narrow shoulder

of this canyon road, glancing
off granite outcroppings, booming

through trees and brush, unstoppable
and heavy as time—which has rotted

upholstery, stripped paint, absorbed
metals until the car fades discretely

into landscape, picked out
only by the occasional hiker

or hunter who, stumbling off the trail,
might circle it, try a door, and then,

stepping back a few yards, pump it full
of .22 caliber holes just for fun.

It might have been any one of us
when we were kids—might have been me

methodically emptying my brother's bolt action
rifle into the hulking remains, loving

the echoing crack of each shot, the smell
and the weight of the weapon pulled tight

against shoulder and cheek, loving especially
the satisfying plunk of the bullet

and the way it would leave the world
forever altered. In any case, the shooter

who riveted a nearly perfect vertical line
all the way up this oil pan's exposed middle

has no doubt forgotten that day
and this car, forgotten how much he wanted

to impress the girl with a kill, how eager
he was, and how somehow he managed

to miss the only shot he'd had all morning
at a single fat quail and its waddling brood.

By now, if he's still alive, he's also forgotten
how after he shot all those holes

into that dead car, he sat with the girl
in the shade of the wreckage and ate

the cheese sandwiches she'd made, drank
water from his canteen, how he told her

his father's war stories, and how the girl
combed her fingers through the grass, retrieving

a handful of empty brass shells, how she
brought one after another to her lips

for a whistle, making him finally
smile before they started the long walk home

empty handed. And now, a generation
later, this eerie white figure stretches

across the oil pan, surrounding the group
of dark holes. This is not the typical spray-painted

work of taggers; this has been brushed on—
or maybe finger-painted—its arms flailing

above its elongated head, and the bullet hole
where the mouth should be gapes

in a kind of scream. The body incorporates
its bullet holes perfectly: head, shoulder, heart

and gut, creating perfect context
after the fact. Another American

teenager has left his mark, the graphic
representation of one man, the violent

means of his death already in place
long before his birth.

Homefront: A Legacy

One front and one battle where everyone in the United
States—every man, woman, and child—is in action.
That front is right here at home, in our daily lives.
      —Franklin Delano Roosevelt, April, 1942

Arizona war worker writes her Navy boyfriend
a thank-you note for the Jap skull he sent her.
      —photo caption, LIFE, 1944

Stationed at her desk, chin resting
pensively in hand, she stares at the skull
almost fondly, almost smiling, as it faces

the camera, hollow-eyed, resting
on its four remaining teeth, lower jaw gone
along with everything else. This soldier has become

a paperweight, a conversation piece
for the blond sweetheart who waits
good-naturedly for her own soldier to return

bringing her picket fence, her station wagon,
her television set. *Here's a good Jap . . . ,*
the handwriting on the skull

begins, and she says: *good.*
Earlier she'd used cuticle scissors to snip
the cord crossed over a box delivered

by the US mail; she peeled off brown paper,
lifted the lid and reached in deep
to pull what was left

of this Japanese soldier from his world
into hers. She might be my mother, or yours,
working days at an Army ordnance depot, listening

to radio news and writing love letters
to her overseas boyfriend after work. But *LIFE*
sent a photographer to catch this

particular moment of tenderness, to document
how unified we are in the effort
of war, the way we stay tightly connected

to each other and our purpose, how the forces
and the homefront resolve to remain
on the same page, and nothing spoils

this picture. She writes: *Thank you darling,*
for the present, and perhaps
she jokes about the impropriety

of accepting this strange man
into her home where she eats and sleeps
and bathes. She refills her pen,

writes: *Hurry home. Hurry*
home to my clean, pressed clothes, to the perfume

of my upswept hair, waved and pinned

with crocheted flowers, my perfectly arched eyebrows,
my beautiful long fingers. She doesn't ask:
who killed this man? Doesn't ask:

who boiled and scraped his head
until it was clean and white enough
to write on? who removed it

from his body? She will never ask: what else
have you done? Right now she is content
to believe in goodness. She doesn't think

of the dead Japanese soldier,
doesn't think of his old mother, bracing for her
long night. She doesn't even think

about what she might do
with this strange souvenir when she tires
of rubbing its round, shiny crown.

At some point she'll need
to stow it out of sight, unfashionable relic
of an old religion—slightly embarrassing,

but indisposable. Silent for years
at a time, the thing will settle back
into her hands without warning

on summer nights when she's washing
her husband's thinning hair, him leaning
awkwardly over the sink, her fingers massaging

his soapy scalp, or it will appear to her
on a bright Arizona morning
when she's shown her son's dental x-ray,

as clear and undeniable as god.
For nearly half a century, the skull
will bide its time, tucked away

in the attic, wrapped discretely
in the daily news like a china teapot,
until someone, maybe

a daughter, pries the lid off
an unlabeled box and recognizes
the efficient blue script

of her dead father's hand
still legible on the bone.

III. Massacre

Mountain Meadow Massacre:
September 11, 1857

*—Who might you find you have come
from yourself if you could trace back
the centuries?*
                    —Walt Whitman

—No pioneer remembrance has been so collectively
repressed than the execution-style murders
of an estimated 120 men, women and children—
California bound emigrants—at the hands
of Mormon zealots . . . .
—Salt Lake Tribune, March 12, 2000

Accidental Revelation: August 1999

. . . It was a very humbling, spiritual experience.
I saw buttons, some pottery, and bones of adults
and children. But the children—that was what
really hit me hard.
        —Washington County Sheriff Kirk Smith

The backhoe is a tool designed to unsettle,
And this one turns up human bones

Like ripe potatoes. Close to 30 bodies rise
To the surface, 30 pounds of broken skeletons, reborn

And ready to loose their tongues
At last. These are specific victims of my own

Ambitious ancestors, who I once believed
Were holy men. The contractor's

First thought is to dump this clattering load
Of bones back into darkness, swearing

His crew to silence. He'd been excavating
Under an old rock cairn in order

To plant the concrete foot
 Of a new memorial, so solid and shiny

It would finally stop a century
Of bleeding. Speeches were written,

Engravings ordered. *Let the book of the past*
Be closed, the prophet would say.

But the dead are not discrete. They refuse
To stay silent. Their awkward arrival

Sets legal process into motion, and forensic
Scientists commence their intimate work

Reconstructing shattered skulls,
Measuring, cataloging, weighing—comparing

Discrepancies with historical reports,
And correspondences to legend

And rumor. Soon, the clamoring
Of the dead grows so loud and insistent

That the governor intercedes—
Though his grandfathers were right there

With mine. He issues an edict
And the nearly known dead

Are swept out of the labs, slipped
Past the ruffled skirts of the law,

And ushered, like municipal waste,
Back underground.

Forensics

The scientist might be bringing her hands
        To a lover's face, the way she picks up this skull
With such tenderness. She's reassembling

Over 2600 pieces of human skeletal remains
        So their stories can finally be heard.
When they are whole enough to speak,

She will translate. These bones
        Were last handled by 19th century soldiers
Who retrieved them from where they'd been

Left to lose their flesh and scatter
        Over a mile or more of Utah wilderness.
Bleached and gnawed by animals and weather,

Long bones were gathered by the armful
        Like crops—or kindling wood—
Before being buried with scraps

Of clothes and clumps of hair pulled
        From low branches and shrubs, beneath a rock
Cairn and a cross. A close-range bullet

Entrance is clearly visible on this forehead,
        And a woman's broken front teeth reveal
That she was shot in the face. A child's skull

Presents a bullet hole at the top of the head,
        And a cranial exit wound on another

Suggests that the killer was looking his victim

Straight in the eye. The scientist confers
      With written reports and testimony, but trusts
Finally in her own fingertips and the bones

Of the dead. This is close physical labor: sorting,
      Labeling and piecing together the tiny shards
Of the scaffolding of someone's face

Or head or forearm; and she works urgently
      Through the night, as if this is an emergency,
As if their *lives* are in her hands,

And just before dawn, she begins
      To coax the first fine threads of truth
From the brittle mouths of the dead.

Unburied

The wicked who fight against Zion
Will surely be smitten at last
  —Mormon hymn

If it's true, that the settlers left the bodies
For wolves and hawks and crows—

That they made only the slightest gesture
Toward burial, tossing ten or twelve

Into a shallow wash, throwing
A few shovels of dirt after them—

What was their reason? Forty men,
Thirty women and close to seventy children

Lay bled-out and naked in the sage brush, waiting
For god, a morbid warning

To future travelers—like the coyotes hung
By a farmer on his barbed wire fence,

Or the raccoons nailed to a post at the edge
Of my grandfather's cornfield. Was it

Simple sloth, the enormity
Of the task and the hard, September dirt?

Or a sudden failure of will in the face
Of what they had done (one man

Saying oddly: I didn't realize
There would be so many)?

Didn't they worry that their own curious
Children, enticed by rumor, might ride out

One afternoon to the site? Or that some
Enterprising photographer might document

This decomposing transgression? It will be
Two years before a US Army regiment

Arrives at the grisly roadside exhibit,
To gather the scattered bones

Into this grave. Until then, the resolute dead
Press on toward their first resurrection,

Becoming the gray wolves that stalk local cattle,
The crows screaming from ragged tops

Of cottonwood trees, the wind howling
Between steep canyon walls, the water

Carving its way through hard valley farms,
And the crisp mountain air

Our fathers and mothers breathe.

Salvage

In the dream, her father kneels
In a dry wash next to the body

Of a ten-year-old boy who lies
Near his mother, both faces

Thick with dirt and dried blood.
Her father might be praying,

But it seems odd how he kneels
At the child's feet, until

She sees him loosen
The leather laces and pull

A small brown boot
Off the left foot and the right.

He ties the boots together and stuffs
Them into a bag, then eases

Off the wool socks and folds
One into the other. When he moves

To the next body, she understands
That this is about utility, that no matter

What happened here,
Her father's god would want

Nothing to go to waste.
The man and his neighbors spend

All day at this grim business, gathering
Livestock, wagons, furniture, bedding,

Pots and pans, and even the clothes
Of the dead. They work quickly, moving

From body to body as if harvesting
Corn or picking peaches, leaving

Nothing but 120 unburied bodies
Who have now paid dearly

For their trespasses. But this is not
In the dream. The girl is awake now

And believes that she can smell
That place, that she can smell death

On her father, asleep in the next room,
And on her mother, whose arm is flung

Tenderly across his chest, and she is afraid—
Not of dying--but that she too

Will learn soon to sleep deeply
Under the salvaged wool blanket

Her mother has washed, hung out
To dry, and spread squarely

Over this narrow bed.

At the Site, With Photo

Everything's wrong here:
The gnarly junipers
Are called cedar trees
By locals, Johnson Fort
Has become the dusty town
Of Enoch, and the meadow is nothing
But a sagebrush flat, stretching
Toward the highway. I walk
Up the steep trail to the ridge, and eat
My dark bread and cheese
With the uncorrected names of the dead
Chattering from the stone wall
At my back. I want to believe
My old cousin returned here
Again and again, sat in this dust,
Eyes closed, listening to the whispers
Rising from these killing fields. I want him
On his knees, want him crying,
Pleading forgiveness
From the ghosts and their god.
But no hint of regret graces
The gaunt, sun-dark face in this photo
Taken a decade after the slaughter
Below this ridge. One of the first
To be raised up in his god's army,
Nephi has become wiry and efficient,
And he will not flinch. He sits here
Stiffly with his rough brothers, staring
Straight through the lens as if it was just
Another unworthy sinner,

One leg crossed high over
The other. I can't see either
Of his hands.

Nephi Johnson: Nightwatch

Nephi was one among many stalwart, valiant
individuals who helped conquer the elements
of this rugged terrain.
          —Hurricane Valley Magazine, 2004

After the massacre is done, you are
Sent back onto the killing field

To spend the night watching over
The property of the dead. The brethren

Have already taken money or pulled watches
From bloodied pockets, rings from fingers,

Hats and boots, but it's late in the day
And your calling is to stay with the spoils

Until morning. Twenty years from now
You will testify that you gave your Indians

Their due, then guarded wagons, carriages,
Quilts, clothing chests, tools, and the sturdy

Pieces of cherrywood furniture flung
Out onto dirt with the corpses. But who was there

To protect it all from? When a shallow moon
Finally floats above the mountains, you can see

Dishes, shoes, iron pots, books, and water buckets

Strewn among scrub oak and salt grass. Feathers

From torn-open bedding sail aimlessly
And gusts of spilled flour sift over sagebrush

In the night air. How will you spend your hours
In this high desert with the newly dead

Slowly cooling all around you? Wrapped
In a blanket listening to your horse

Breathe and stamp as he shifts position
In the dark, you might stare upward

At the bright western sky in time to see
A Perseid meteor streaking

Its incomprehensible message
Across heaven. Perhaps you simply walk

Among the dead, counting them, touching
One now and then, just to be sure

They are gone for good. You have become
The unlikely custodian of the future,

And you have created your legacy—
Which you will pass on to me and mine as silently

As cancer or a heart defect—but tonight,

Barely twenty years old, you will

Simply take inventory with rifle in hand,
Build a small, efficient fire against the chill

And the gathering wolves, and lie down
Among the slaughtered, on this earth.

Fruit From a Tree in Zion: Rosemary Johnson

> *. . . bones make good fertilizer; a few bones at*
> *the roots of a tree would nourish it a long time.*
> *As for the cursed mobocrats, I can think of nothing*
> *better that they could do than to feed a fruit tree in Zion.*
> —Mormon Apostle George A Smith,
> Cedar City, Utah Territory, August 1857

If the girl allows herself to believe
That it wasn't an Indian massacre—that it was
Her own uncles, brothers, and cousins

Who slaughtered the travelers, who stole
Wagons, cattle, children, who left
The meadow littered with rotting corpses—

The sun will fall screaming
From the sky. She hears the late-night
Murmering of father and brothers

Around the heavy pine table, and she listens
To the red-haired neighbor girl's
Secrets. Her mother slaps her face, says: *Silence*

Is the midwife of obedience, says:
You are blessed. You are the ripening
Fruit from a tree in Zion, and she prays

For rain to cleanse the land
Of its sins and its questions. But whispers
Rise and fly through the night like dark

Swallows, and the girl opens
Her bedroom window. She leans out,
Listening, and waits for the cold rain

To fall. Years later,
Her grandchildren will stand
In these same dry fields watching

Pink clouds of radioactive dust hover
Over their houses and crops, dusting
Their livestock and their children's blond hair,

And they will ask no questions, say: *nothing
Is wrong here.* They will believe
In necessity, swallowing their bitter secrets

With their boiled potatoes and peas,
Waiting for rain, atomic nightmares
Exploding in their silent hearts.

Survivors

My father was killed by Indians; when they
washed their faces, they were white men.
　　　—Christopher Carson Fancher, child survivor

. . . and many generations shall not pass away
among them, save they shall be a white
and a delightsome people.
　　　—Book of Mormon prophecy regarding
　　　American Indians

The smallest are pulled
　　　From their mothers'
Dead bodies and loaded
　　　Into a wagon, one ragged arm
Dangling, nearly severed
　　　At the elbow, one shot
Through her ear by the same
　　　Bullet that killed her father,
All of them shrieking and smeared
　　　With dirt and the blood
Of their brothers, sisters,
　　　Mothers, fathers. One will say:
I saw my mother shot
　　　In the forehead and fall
Dead. One will say: *You don't forget*
　　　The horror . . . . You don't forget
The screaming. And she will say:
　　　You wouldn't forget it, either,
If you saw your own

Mother topple over
In the wagon beside you,
With a red splotch getting bigger
On the front of her calico dress.
Another will remember
How the killers were disguised
As Indians, how they
Went to the creek and washed
The paint from their faces.
Seventeen children
Are hauled off the fields
To a ranch where the saints
Who spared them as *too young*
To tell the tale, distribute them
Like sacks of flour or allotments
Of seed grain among the brethren.
For two years you live in silence
With your captors, learning
To bow your head before
Their almighty god who prevailed
So completely over your parents'
Distant god—the one who hasn't
Seemed to notice the plain pioneer
Woman you call *Sister* wearing your
Mother's good winter coat, doesn't
Notice your dead uncle's
Smart black carriage rattling
Through the rough streets
Of Cedar City, or that familiar
Gold watch shining in the palm

Of the same holy hand
That drew a hunting knife across
        Your brother's ten-year-old throat.
So you wait for your god's
        Late arrival, and you begin
To believe, in the lifetime before
        The US Army delivers you,
That you might have witnessed
        A miracle the day you saw Indians
Transformed into white men, saw them
        Kneeling at the creek, washing
Their faces and bodies, saw
        The dark color leave their skin, slide
Down their arms along with the blood
        Of your parents, stream
Awkwardly from their elbows into
        The same cold rush of water
That fills their buckets
        And feeds their crops.

Wife

Could the settler's wife be so hungry
For new shoes, for a scrap of lace, for the blue
Flowered dress, that she wouldn't ask

Where did it come from? Wouldn't ask
Whose was it? Who removed it
From her body? Did you

Close her eyelids with your fingertips
Before you turned her
To loose the buttons

One by one from her neck
All the way down past her waist? Did you
Touch her hair? Did you ease her

Left arm out of its sleeve first, the way you do
Mine, late at night, in the cool dark
Of our bedroom? Did you raise her hips

To slide the dress down, careful
Not to tear the fabric
As you drew it finally past her

Legs, past her pale bare feet? And then,
When you reached around to untie
The petticoats' drawstring at the waist,

Easing each of the under-layers
Over her hips, were you

Thinking of me? Were you thinking

Of me stepping into those white ruffles, running
A finger along the embroidered hem?
And when your fingers touched

The skin of her belly, her breasts, when you pushed
The last under-dress up around her
Shoulders, bending each arm at the elbow

To free it as if you were undressing
One of the children for a bath, when you forced
The baggy flannel over her head—

Which you must have been holding
In your left hand for that moment—while her
Face was hidden, making her appear

Uninjured, even beautiful, stripped bare
Under the birds and the September sun,
Were you thinking of me?

IV. Trajectory

City Cemetery Love Poem: 1975

The spirit of God like a fire is burning . . .
—William W. Phelps, from a Mormon hymn

Make Love, Not War!
—1960s protest slogan

We've walked a long time, talking and holding
hands among blue shadows, putting a little distance
between us and our noisy friends, whose voices

and guitar music trail us around smoky corners, along
city sidewalks until we climb over
the stone wall and enter this pine and cedar

sanctuary. We walk into the heart,
past the dancing angel statue, past the Catholic section
and the mausoleum, to the oldest ancestors, who must know

we mean no dishonor when we stop to rest
and share a fat joint at the resting place
of William Phelps, revered justice of the peace and poet

of hymns, whose stone reads: *There is no end*
to glory/ There is no end to love/ There is
no end to being/ There is no death

above. We begin to kiss and touch
each other's faces, right there
on that grave's long grass, and when the moon breaks

full and high above the trees, and Utah's bright
September stars scatter themselves thickly, we fall
into each other's arms, pulling off

our shoes and shirts and pants, and loving
the mountain air and the quiet of the grave and the sense
that we are somehow bringing joy to the ancient

bones beneath us. We're so deep into our own
nerve endings that we don't even hear the helicopter
until it is directly overhead, and we laugh as it circles

the cemetery, making its loud *whop, whop, whop.*
That's the sound of war, you shout
into my ear. *We should continue*

making love—which we do—with gusto—
and when the helicopter comes back around, a white
spotlight descends like the finger of god

just at the right moment, and we fall apart
laughing, and look up, breathless and happy
and naked, surrounded by the angelic circle

of light that levitates us a few feet above good
Brother Phelps. We feel blessed, floating
between worlds, utterly untouchable

by anyone above or below. When the helicopter
turns off its spotlight and angles up and away, our bodies

move back together, your hands warm

on my face and my back, our sighs
and murmurs once again audible among the dead.
But it's the barking of dogs in the distance

that pulls us apart this time, and we are suddenly aware
of a megaphone-enhanced police voice blaring
from the east wall and the clamor

of fanatical dogs advancing angrily
in our direction. We leap to our feet and become
two streakers, grabbing our strewn clothes, running

south, dodging angels and other icons
as we try to stick arms through tangled sleeves,
brush off pine needles, and the dogs

get louder, and I drop a shoe, as I jump a low
gravestone, and we dash, naked track stars, trailing underwear
and calling to each other, and I think about

the consequences, because technically I'm still married
to someone else, though the marriage is truly over, but I know
we'll be embarrassed, and they will search us

for drugs—and they will find them—because neither of us thought
to toss the extra joint from your shirt pocket—and your family
will hate me, and what about our jobs, and my children

will think I'm a bad mother—or worse—but we keep running
across all those restive bones, and by some miracle
we stay ahead of the flashlights and the amplified voices

and the insane dogs, and we hurdle that last wall
onto the 4th Avenue sidewalk, joining hands
descending, alive.

Dead Finch in the Parsley

I know it's a finch by the fat triangle
of its beak, collapsed on a heap
of feathers and bones and what's left
of flesh. Its last effort
must have been a panicky flutter—
if birds can feel panic—over the lip
of this clay pot, and under this thicket
of overgrown parsley, escaping
the claws of the neighbor's cat
too late to do any good. I scoop it out
with a wooden spoon, and look at it
for a long time. I don't know
what I'm looking for—but not this
transitory creature, no longer bird,
not yet soil. My mother
used to bury fish under her roses,
and I imagined them swimming
among roots, which were swimming
themselves, pushing their thin fingers
out and down through
their dark world, consuming
everything on their way to bearing
what we know as roses
above ground. What is it
about the in-between
that frightens us? Maggots
swarming over garbage, the fat grub
turned up by a garden spade,
the chrysalis broken open
by a cat, the unexpected pulpy mass

inside the occasional fresh egg—we cringe
even at the dark oozing of a peach
left too long on the sill. Some days
grief inhabits our lives
as a terrible longing
for form, immutable and discrete,
and though I tell myself *nature*
and tell myself *cycle*, today
I want my dead brother back whole
and twenty years old, in his familiar body,
unambiguous as a rose, and today
I find no comfort in the grass
beneath my feet or the parsley
I chop and scatter
over steamed potatoes and butter.

Trajectory

1.   Las Vegas Medical Center, Trauma Unit: Chairs

We're allowed 20 minutes every 2 hours.
A buzzer unlocks the steel security door
each time. In between, we watch
the television mounted high on the wall
at one end of the room. On a promo
for Channel 4 News, a man we love is transferred
from ambulance to helicopter over and over.
We can't change the channel. It shows
a local child and the dog that bit her. It says
the dog has been destroyed. And now—
that little girl's bloody, dog-bitten body,
covered with emergency equipment, is wheeled
right past us into surgery. It's eerie—
the nightly news bursting its way
through these doors where we wait.

2.   Gunshot

The bullet entered just above the mouth,
the right side of the face. It slammed
through the jaw, the facial nerve,
into the zygomatic bone and the temporal,
just at the jaw's hinge point, splintering there
to send shrapnel tearing into the ear canal

and out of the head, biting off a substantial piece

«85»

of the outer ear as it left. It was a nine millimeter.
That was its size. The larger part of the slug
deflected inward toward the base
of the brain, coming to rest just in time
under the cerebellum, just past
the top of the spine, where the last vertebrae
feeds the spinal cord into the brain.

3.   Critical Care Nurse

In a few days, the farmer with the gunshot wound
will begin to weave in and out
of consciousness. Each time he wakes,

he won't remember, and we'll have to tell him
over and over again what happened. Each time,
it will tear him apart. Sometimes I wish

they'd stay asleep. It's not the blood
or the dismemberment or even the death
that gets to me. It's the terror.

These beds are always inhabited
by terror. People are afraid of what they remember,
afraid of what they don't, and most afraid

of what will happen next. When I have time,

I hold their hands. This farmer's hands
are so callused, you can't prick his finger

with a needle—they're like the soles
of my feet in summer—they seem like armor—
invincible hands. The morphine is giving him

nightmares. He will tell us when he can
that he dreamed of shiny metal shards,
rows and rows of gleaming steel rods. He will say

it was horrible—threatening—unbearable.
This is common. I can reduce the dose,
but he will feel more pain. The little girl

of the pit bull attack will be up and walking
this week. She's had titanium
replacements for broken bones

in her face. There will be many surgeries.
Her parents have been told she will make
full recovery. The gang girl

will die. Most patients die. Her body
will be removed and her boyfriend will be
watched by police. New traumas

arrive. These beds are always full. We buzz
families in and out of the waiting room.
We tell them what we can.

4.	Chairs: Middle of the Night

Everyone here is cold. We wrap ourselves
in blankets and jackets and wait to hear
if anyone will live: the teenaged girlfriend
shot by rival gang kids, the three-year-old daughter
mauled by a neighbor's pit bull, the brother blasted
from his Harley Davidson straight through
the windshield of the pickup truck that hit him,
the dairy farmer shot in the face
by a distraught employee. There are armed guards
at the door who sign us in and out, checking
photo IDs each time, and a policeman
questions the friends of the gang girl
one at a time. It occurs to me
that they are nearly old enough
to go to war. The policeman wears
a nine-millimeter handgun
in a leather holster on his belt.

5.	Volunteer Ambulance Crew

We found them in a heap, the shooter
lying partially on top of the survivor
in front of the milking barn. I thought
they were both dead. It was my son's first
emergency run—he'd just finished training
the week before. We took vitals and found

a pulse on the farmer, but it looked to me
like an exit wound
on the back of his head. There was a voice
coming from his body—a radio
buckled to his belt. I could hear a boy:
Dad, come in Dad. What's going on

out there? Where are you? We heard sirens.
Dad—come in. The boy wouldn't stop,
and we couldn't answer, but later I thought
maybe that child's voice
is what kept this guy alive—his son
calling him back from wherever
that bullet was sending him.

6.   Witness

Did you know he brought a gun to work?

Yes—I mean it doesn't surprise me. Lots of guys carry guns.

Did you hear anything unusual that night?

No—the radio was playing Mexican music in the milking barns as
usual, and then there was some yelling. But nothing I worried about.

Didn't you hear the first shot?

Yes, but there are gunshots around here all the time. We shoot rats,
dogs, coyotes, whatever. I thought nothing of it until I heard him
yell he'd killed the boss.

What did you do then?

I ran toward the barn, but he'd already shot himself by the time
I got there, so I called 911 and stayed till the ambulance came.

What do you think happened?

He shot the boss, then he shot himself.

Were there any problems between the two men?

No. Just the usual—one works for the other.

7.   Trauma Unit: Beds

His head is swollen beyond
recognition, and his jaw has been

wired shut. I've never seen anyone
so badly bruised. His hair

is partially shaved, his wrists
strapped to bed rails. A breathing tube
threads through a messy hole, cut quickly

into the base of his throat. The bullet hole

on the stretched skin of his face
is unbandaged and no bigger

than a dime. A pair of wire cutters
hangs on the wall. They tell us he is not

in a coma; they tell us
it's a coma-like state.

Blue tubes enter and exit
his body and a monitor beeps

graphs and numbers. Everything
is being recorded. This bed

is number 6. There are 12 beds
total. The wound

on the back of his skull is not
an exit wound. We are told

it's a simple cut
from the fall—10 stitches—

like the gash he got last year
when he slipped in his shower.

They tell us he is lucky. They say

he has no permanent damage.

There's a television talking
in the corner. What's left

of the bullet nuzzles right
up close to the brain.

—for RB and MB

Unsolved

Hikers discover the car, windows blasted out,
lovers' bodies slouching easily in the backseat as if
napping, except for the blood and the fact

that their faces had been blown apart.
I knew the woman—she'd never married after
that short first time, and only

after her accidental daughter
was safely grown had she allowed herself
this luxury of romance. At first I imagine

the killer as monster—an animal that must feel
nothing recognizably human. But after all this time,
police haven't found him, and it occurs to me

that the killer is just another person—he might be
any one of us, shopping at the bakery, picking out oranges
at a fruit stand or waiting in line behind me

at the bank to cash his check. The problem is
who to be afraid of. After he went crazy
the last time, my father would sit for hours

in a state hospital lawn chair, observing
passing traffic. Whenever he heard the screaming
siren of an approaching ambulance, he'd smile

and say: *another dog dead,*
marking an imaginary score card
in the air. I'd tell myself to pay

no attention—he wasn't in his right mind. His brain
had been zapped twice: once by the heat
of his own body, trying its best

to burn out an infection; and once
by medical doctors trying to burn out
the source of his rage. But it was my father

at his sanest who taught me to favor humans,
never allowing pets in the house, drowning
all those unwanted kittens in the ditch

at the end of the road, and ending the suffering
of an ailing dog with a cold bullet to the brain.
The woman's glasses were still sprawled

on the dash of the car and there was a Colorado roadmap
stretched open across the front seat, held down
by an unopened water bottle and a gaping

grease-stained bag of potato chips. The man's
mud-crusted boots and a leather camera case lay empty
on the floor. The woman's daughter imagines

these details whenever she drives her own car. She'll stop
for nothing. She passes hitch-hikers, stranded
motorists, even accidents, without so much as lifting

her foot off the gas. Her children strapped safely
to the back seat, these days she carries

a gun in her bag within reach. The investigating officer

said it didn't look personal. The couple
simply got in the path of someone else's storm.
My father smokes and rocks in his plastic chair,

braiding facts from our lives
into stories of persecution and faith and significance,
and I listen, nodding and lighting

the next cigarette between his lips. A California wildfire
is blazing on television when I get home and I see
trees and houses and sheds and stables crackling

into ash. One man has died, a news voice tells me, burned
to oblivion while saving his mangy cat, and by tomorrow
there will be two more, incinerated in their car

as they sleep. And this wildfire isn't wild
at all. It's the deliberate blistering rage
of a single human being, sweeping across

highways, orchards, swimming pools, gathering
strength as it consumes house after house, swooping
low through a narrow canyon and rising, sucking

up everything in its path and raining it all back down
in blackened bits that dissolve
into nothing at our touch.

Firewood

A boy is stacking two full cords, carrying
      each split log in his skinny arms
from the driveway, where the old farm woman
      whose husband's recent stroke has left her
alone in this business, dumped them
      haphazardly before dawn. When he left
for school, it looked like a giant scrap heap
      of dead leaves and oversized toy logs—like the remains
of one of those elaborate structures
      he and his friends would blow up or knock down
shortly after construction. Now his mother's
      red Ford Escort slouches stupidly
behind the scrambled logs where the tow truck
      cut it loose, tilting heavily toward the driver's side
where tires collapse against bent rims
      and the red metal of the body cringes,
bashed in like a crushed loaf of bread. His mother
      was sideswiped today by a truck.
She was knocked unconscious right there
      at the driver's window, which is now
just a few haggard shards clinging
      to the edges of its frame. He is stacking the wood
neatly, in the sturdy, overlapping design
      his father taught him, on the porch still stained
with the blood of a fat cardinal
      his cat had emphatically torn to pieces
in front of him last week. The boy works
      without resting, without even smelling
the fresh split cherry or walnut, sculpting the stack
      as he goes, each pie-shaped end facing out

and pointing the same direction, a monument
        of firewood rising to his own height, against
the dark, west wall of the house where his mother leans
        from her upstairs bedroom window, calling
that she is fine, that he should take a break.
        But he doesn't look up. He keeps stacking
and stacking, as if it were art—as if it weren't meant,
        after all, to be burned.

                        —for JTB

Failed Blessing

—for my daughter, waiting for the birth of her child

I want to give you an oak tree grown
from the perfect acorn we found
where it had fallen on the poet's grave
in your eighth month, or a scrap
of embroidery done by the young hand
of your great-grandmother. My house
is scattered with starts: the sprouting
acorn in one pot, a rose cutting
from my childhood home
in another, a half-crocheted
lavender blanket, stacks of quilt squares
cut from remnants of your well-worn
clothes, a box of old photos,
a letter, a poem, but none of this
feels right. How can I help
bring this child from your body
into the world of air and time? Here
in this dark kitchen, Mars looming
close and cold at the window, I'm
as helpless as I have ever been,
and I think of nights when you were
small and sick—your damp hair
coiling at the soft nape
of your neck, your breathing
as raspy and unreliable as the dark clock
on the table, and I believed
I could save you if I held you close
and long enough. I want to take back the pain

you felt then, the fear and nightmares
and all the other wounds and losses
I've been able to do nothing
to prevent or mend. I want to paint them
pale and thin into the background—
those accidental gifts
of grief I bestowed
with your birth. I want you
to wrap them up like laundry
and send them back to me
in brown paper, and I will cut
the strings and open the bundle
slowly, unfolding each injury, each
slight, each death, each illness, each
unresolved dread, and I will wear them
next to my own old skin, rough,
unwashed, undone.

Clarity: Because I'm Not There

I imagine my sister nudging our mother
out of bed, easing her breakable body
down the hallway. At the bathroom door

my sister offers help, but she waits
until our mother nods yes, that she'd like a hand
getting out of her wet nightclothes, washing

her body, pulling on the clean cotton underwear
my sister has ready in her pocket. They eat
their oatmeal together at a glass table

in a sunny plant-filled room with tall, clean
windows instead of walls, watching squirrels
and birds at the feeders, and the trees moving

in the wind beyond them, and the houses and hills
beyond the trees. My sister has scattered
sunflower seeds along the railing to draw

more birds, and once in a while, our mother
will look up and point out a nuthatch
or a downy woodpecker, and for a moment,

she will seem almost happy. Soon my sister will lean
into her chair, right up close, their faces
nearly touching, and I'll know they are breathing

each other's breath. My sister will speak
kindly, coax our mother to drink more water,

a sip of tea or juice, explain why she needs her

to get dressed, why she needs to pull herself
into the car again, snap the tense safety belt
around her hips, then make her way across

the new hospital's hot asphalt parking lot, through
the steamy southern air, through the thick glass
doors. One of them will push the elevator button

and they will step into the glass box
that will carry them up three floors
to the infusion room, where our mother

sinks with no coaxing at all into the dark
reclining chair, offers up her right arm, and waits
for whatever sweet trickle of hope

that clear tube might convey. My sister brings
yogurt, water, a banana, a stack
of magazines, and they wait together

until the drip stops and a nurse removes
the needle, presses a cotton ball
over the wound and a see-through band-aid

over that. Everything has become transparent—
the elevator, the doors, the water glass, even this
stupid band-aid with our mother's blood

blossoming beneath it. In the evening,
my sister loads her CD player with oldies
and they look at photos of family or watch

hummingbirds frantically sparring
for sugar water—all urgency and flutter—
and our mother smiles, and my sister snaps

photos, and they listen to the twangy buzz
of cicadas until the sun begins its steep slide
behind the dark hills. When our mother

starts to doze, head sagging sideways
in her chair, my sister will linger
with her camera by the tall window

saying: *Mama, don't fall asleep yet—*
stay up awhile. She'll say: *Wait with me.*
I think there's still enough light

for another hummingbird—and another.

—for JN

Late Summer Moratorium

This week I refuse to let anything die.
I water twice a day when it's hot, pluck
fat, green worms off geraniums

and set them onto a pile of fresh
prunings. I take cuttings
from a leggy coleus, slide crisp stems

into a full water glass where they begin
to generate thin white filaments,
reproducing their own bodies

as I watch. I brush ants from the walk
with a soft broom and leave spiders
to their own dusky work in corners

and cracks. This week even the greedy
snails will survive: one by one I carry them
on the flat of my hand to a damp corner

near the fence. I drink my morning coffee
close to an open window, ready
to scare bluejay or crow from the nervous

hatchling dove balanced in a tangle of twigs
above the porch, and ready to startle
the neighbor's sleek cat when she creeps

too near the fish pond in my yard. I spend
long hours separating goldfish eggs and fry

from their efficient parents,

who would eat them in a minute,
given half a chance. How do any of us live
in such a world? I've grown so tired

of the dead. They are so much work—
and they never sleep. I'm afraid
I won't be able to care

for even one more. I've got too many
dead with me already, crowding
and pushing their way inside—as if

they have nowhere else to go—as if
there is no difference at all
between heaven and the human heart.

The Autumn House Poetry Series

Michael Simms, General Editor

OneOnOne · Jack Myers
Snow White Horses · Ed Ochester
The Leaving: New and Selected Poems · Sue Ellen Thompson
Dirt · Jo McDougall
Fire in the Orchard · Gary Margolis
The White Calf Kicks · Deborah Slicer ◊ 2003
The Divine Salt · Peter Blair
The Dark Takes Aim · Julie Suk
Satisfied with Havoc · Jo McDougall
Half Lives · Richard Jackson
Not God After All · Gerald Stern
(with drawings by Sheba Sharrow)
Dear Good Naked Morning · Ruth L. Schwartz ◊ 2004
Collected Poems · Patricia Dobler
Déjà Vu Diner · Leonard Gontarek
lucky wreck · Ada Limón ◊ 2005
The Golden Hour · Sue Ellen Thompson
The Autumn House Anthology of Contemporary American Poetry
       · Sue Ellen Thompson, ed.
Woman in the Painting · Andrea Hollander Budy
Joyful Noise: An Anthology of American Spiritual Poetry · Robert Strong, ed.
No Sweeter Fat · Nancy Pagh ◊ 2006
Unreconstructed: Poems Selected and New · Ed Ochester

Design and Production

Design by Erik Rosen

Cover Art: *Utah House* © 2011 by Jackie Clegg Nielson

Title and text font: Lucida Sans Regular, designed by Charles Bigelow and Kris Holmes in 1985.

Printed by McNaughton-Gunn on 60# Natural Offset.